Contents

Learn
Drop
Stitch
Crochet™

Introduction

I have always been fascinated with drop stitches in handknitting and have longed for the ability to use drop stitches in crochet. I've experimented with several different methods, but this method has been the one that has worked the best for me.

Although this method resembles broomstick lace in its mechanics, it is actually a fringing technique, which I discovered in a book from the 1970s. This method would produce fringe by cutting the strands after completion. Although I didn't explore that technique, what I discovered is that when used in the body of the fabric, I had beautiful drop stitches, which stayed put after completion!

Once you've gone through the tutorial section, you'll have eight projects on which to practice and master your new skill.

These projects require the use of a knitting needle to maintain consistency of the drop stitch height. Using a smaller diameter needle will produce smaller drops, while using a larger diameter needle will produce larger drops. I have chosen only two sizes of knitting needles for these projects to allow you to complete several of the projects with the same needle.

I recommend natural fibers for all of the drop stitch projects because blocking significantly improves the finished look of the drop stitches.

You'll certainly want to make the projects the best they can be. Blocking can be as simple as laying the project flat and shaping it before allowing it to dry. The use of pins is optional. Like me, you may decide that pinning is unnecessary.

There are so many natural animal fibers available today—wool, superwash wool, alpaca, camel, etc.—as well as plant-based yarns, such as cotton, linen, bamboo, milk and more. These projects will allow you the opportunity to try these new yarns while making some extraordinary projects.

While I was working on this book, I was also researching grape varieties for my garden. It turns out that grape varieties have beautiful names, and I decided to use those names for the projects in this book. I wanted to add a little bit of myself to the book.

—Kim Guzman

Tutorial

To get started with drop stitch crochet, you'll first want to practice your stitches. You'll need a crochet hook and a knitting needle to learn this technique. It will take practice, so don't get discouraged. As with all new techniques, you will need to allow yourself time to learn before you jump into a project.

MAKING A DROP STITCH

To practice, start with something small. Start by making a length of 16 chains. Skip the first chain and single crochet in each remaining chain. You will have 15 single crochet (*Photo 1*).

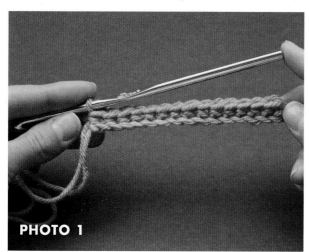

PHOTO 1

Without turning your work, chain 1. Using your non-hook hand, hold the knitting needle close to your work. The knitting needle will be pointing in the direction of your work (pointing to the right for right-handers or pointing to the left for left-handers) (*Photo 2*).

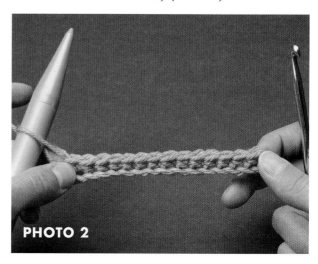

PHOTO 2

Extend the loop on your hook until it is large enough to fit on the knitting needle and place it on the needle (*Photo 3*).

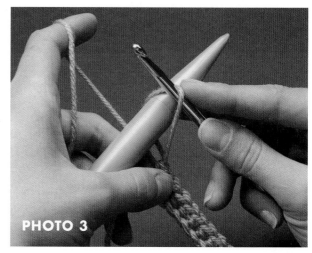

PHOTO 3

The first drop stitch is now on your needle and is in the position of the first single crochet of the row below. To make the next drop stitch, insert your hook in the second single crochet from the needle *(Photo 4)*, yarn over and pull up a loop and chain 1.

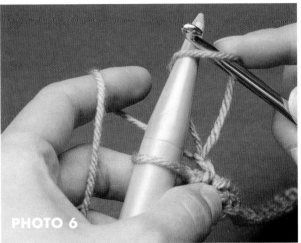

PHOTO 6

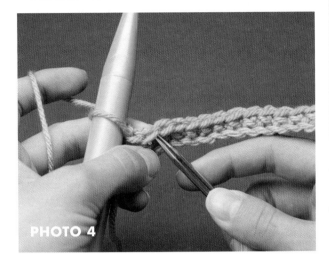

PHOTO 4

Move the loops down the length of the knitting needle as work progresses.

When placing drop stitches on the knitting needle, ensure that you are placing them at the widest part of the needle in order to maintain a consistent height *(Photo 7)*.

Extend the loop on your hook until it is large enough to fit on the knitting needle and place it on the needle *(Photos 5 and 6)*.

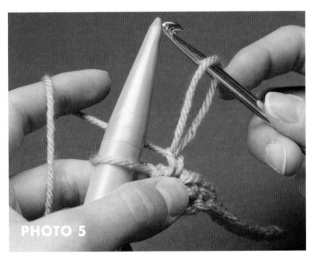

PHOTO 5

PHOTO 7

If you place them only at the tip of the needle, they will not move freely as work progresses. If necessary, tighten the drop stitch gently after placement, but generally, pulling up the next drop stitch will tighten the prior drop stitch.

If a pattern indicates that you will be working in the back loop only, it means the loop of the stitch that is farthest away from you (*see illustration b*). If a pattern indicates that you will be working in the front loop only, it means the loop of the stitch closest to you (*see illustration a*). If there is no indication, it means that you will work under both loops of the single crochet (*see illustration c*).

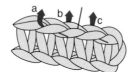

Front Loop (a)
Back Loop (b)
Both Loops (c)

Continue making drop stitches in each single crochet. Be sure to count your drop stitches while on the needle (*Photo 8*). Ensure that you have 15 (*the same number of single crochet*).

PHOTO 8

If you have more or fewer drop stitches, try again. Inspect the stitches closely to ensure that you have the correct number.

Once you have made all your drop stitches and you have the correct number, carefully slide the stitches off the knitting needle (*Photos 9 and 10*).

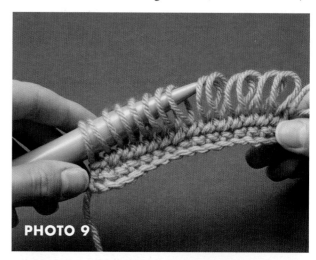

PHOTO 9

PHOTO 10

Do not worry about the stitches. Remember that there is a chain at the bottom of each drop stitch. This stabilizes the stitch, allowing you to work with it without the needle in place. We suggest that you do not leave the drop stitches on the needle for long periods of time or put your project in your project bag while the stitches are on the needle. But, the drop stitches will be stable for long enough to allow you to stitch into them.

COMPLETING THE DROP STITCHES

Now that you've made your drop stitches, you'll need to complete the stitches on the next row. Again, you won't turn your work to begin.

Extend the yarn until it reaches the height of the drop stitch. Use care on this first drop stitch. Although the stitches are relatively stable, the first one can increase or decrease in height easily. Try to maintain the same height when you are leaving the length of yarn.

Insert your hook in the first drop stitch *(Photo 11)*, yarn over, pull a loop through, chain 1 *(Photo 12)*.

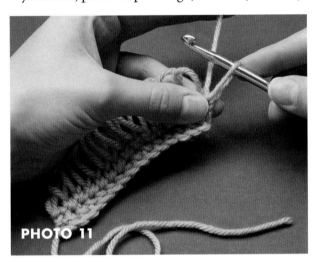

PHOTO 11

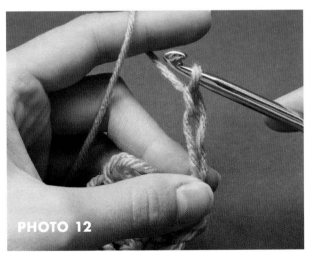

PHOTO 12

Single crochet in the same drop stitch *(Photo 13)*.

PHOTO 13

To continue, work single crochet in each remaining drop stitch *(Photo 14)*. Use care to ensure that the drop stitch isn't twisted.

PHOTO 14

Continue practicing by repeating the drop stitch row and the single crochet row alternately until you feel comfortable enough to start a project. It may take some time to develop your own style in holding the knitting needle while crocheting with your hook hand. Give yourself some time to discover what suits you best.

WORKING WITH A GREATER NUMBER OF STITCHES

There are times when you'll be working with more stitches than will fit on the knitting needle or when you are working in the round. In these instances, you will work your row or round in sections. Fill the knitting needle with drop stitches. Once you have a comfortable number of drop stitches on the hook or once you can no longer work drop stitches in the round, you can easily remove the stitches you've made and then continue making more drop stitches.

When you've made the number of drop stitches you desire and need to remove them in order to continue, carefully slide them off the knitting needle. Replace the last 3 or 4 drop stitches on the needle in order to maintain stability; continue making drop stitches across (Photo 15).

PHOTO 15

MAKING A CROSS-STITCH

To make a cross-stitch in drop stitch crochet, you will be crossing the drop stitches and working them out of order. In the Sultana Scarf, the cross-stitch consists of 3 drop stitches crossed behind 3 other drop stitches.

To work this cross-stitch, skip the next 3 drop stitches and work a single crochet into each of the next 3 drop stitches, allowing the skipped drop stitches to remain in the front of your work (Photos 16 and 17).

PHOTO 16

PHOTO 17

Now work a single crochet into each of the
skipped drop stitches beginning with the first
skipped dropped stitch *(Photos 18 and 19)*.

PHOTO 18

PHOTO 19

MAKING A TWISTED DROP STITCH

Ordinarily, you will want to ensure that your
stitch isn't twisted before you complete a drop
stitch. However, in the Perlette Cowl, you will
be purposely making twisted drop stitches.
The twist is made after all the drop stitches
have been made.

On your practice piece, insert your hook into
the first drop stitch as you would normally
(Photo 20).

PHOTO 20

Twist your hook in order to twist the drop stitch
360 degrees *(Photos 21–24)*.

PHOTO 21

PHOTO 22

PHOTO 23

PHOTO 24

Now, extend the yarn up to the height of the drop stitch, yarn over, pull the loop through and chain 1. Complete the stitch with a single crochet *(Photo 25)*.

PHOTO 25

Next, insert the hook in the next drop stitch *(Photo 26)*,

PHOTO 26

twist hook 360 degrees *(Photos 27–30)*,

PHOTO 27

PHOTO 30

single crochet in the same stitch *(Photo 31)*.

PHOTO 28

PHOTO 31

Continue across the piece, twisting each drop stitch before working the single crochet into it. When you have finished, you should have 15 twisted drop stitches *(Photo 32)*. ∎

PHOTO 32

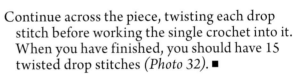

PHOTO 29

Mireille *Wrap*

SKILL LEVEL
◼◼◻◻
EASY

FINISHED MEASUREMENTS
17 inches x 69 inches at widest points

MATERIALS
- Universal Yarn Fibra Natura Flax light (light worsted) weight linen yarn (1¾ oz/137 yds/50g per hank): 6 hanks #12 tarragon
- Size I/9/5.5mm crochet hook or size needed to obtain gauge
- Size 19 (15mm) desired length knitting needle
- Tapestry needle

GAUGE
In pattern: 21 sts = 4 inches (blocked); rows 1–7 = 3 inches (blocked)

PATTERN NOTES
Linen is a lovely summer-weight fiber, but it will feel a little stiff in use. It is the nature of linen. The fiber tends to soften over time.

Drop stitches are created left-to-right for right-handers or right-to-left for left-handers.

As the knitting needle becomes full of loops, gently remove the loops and replace the needle in the last 3 or 4 worked loops to maintain consistency and continue working drop stitches for remainder of row (see page 8).

SPECIAL STITCH
Drop stitch (drop st): Hold knitting needle in non-hook hand close to work with point facing direction of work. Insert hook as indicated, yo, pull lp through, ch 1, extending lp on hook to fit over knitting needle, place lp on needle (see page 4).

WRAP
Row 1: With crochet hook, ch 90, sc in 2nd ch from hook, sc in each of next 5 chs, *3 sc in next ch, sc in each of next 5 chs, sk next 2 chs, sc in each of next 5 chs, rep from * to last 6 chs, 3 sc in next ch, sc in each of next 5 chs, turn.

Row 2: Ch 1, working in **front lp** (*see Stitch Guide*), sk first sc, sc in each of next 5 sc, *3 sc in next sc, sc in each of next 5 sc, sk next 2 sc, sc in each of next 5 sc, rep from * to last 7 sc, 3 sc in next sc, sc in each of next 4 sc, sk next sc, sc in last sc, turn.

Rows 3–5: Rep row 2. At end of last row, **do not turn.**

Row 6: Holding knitting needle in non-hook hand, close to work, ch 1, extending lp on hook to fit over needle, place lp on needle (*first drop st made*), working in **back lp** (*see Stitch Guide*), work **drop st** (*see Special Stitch*) in each rem sc across, remove all drop sts from knitting needle. **Do not turn.** (*91 drop sts*)

Row 7: Leaving small length of yarn to match height of drop st (see page 7), insert hook in first drop st, yo, pull lp through, ch 1, sc in same drop st, sc in each rem drop st across, turn. (*91 sc*)

Row 8: Rep row 2.

Note: *Use special care not to count beg ch of previous row as a st.*

Rows 9–11: Rep row 2. At end of last row, do not turn.

Rows 12–137: [Rep rows 6–11 consecutively]
21 times. At end of last row, fasten off.

BLOCKING
Immerse project in cool water, squeeze to remove
excess water, roll in clean towel to remove as
much water as possible, lay flat and shape,
stretching out the drop sts to their full height.
Allow to dry. ∎

Vanessa *Jacket*

SKILL LEVEL

⬛⬛⬛⬜
EXPERIENCED

FINISHED SIZES

Instructions given fit 32–38-inch bust *(small/ medium)*; changes for 40–48-inch bust *(large/ X-large)* are in [ ].

MATERIALS

- Plymouth Yarn DK Merino Superwash light (light worsted) weight superwash merino wool yarn (1¾ oz/130 yds/50g per ball):
    5 [8] balls #1117 light grey
- Size H/8/5mm crochet hook or size needed to obtain gauge
- Size 17 (12.75mm) desired length knitting needle
- Tapestry needle

GAUGE

16 sts = 4 inches (blocked); 4 rows = 2 inches (blocked)

PATTERN NOTES

Garment begins at back of shoulders and is worked from top down; for the front, stitches are picked up in unused loops of foundation row and worked down. The front and back are then joined and the body is worked in one piece from top down.

Due to this fiber's ability to block, garment can be blocked to accommodate a range of sizes.

Drop stitches are created left-to-right for right-handers or right-to-left for left-handers.

As the knitting needle becomes full of loops, gently remove the loops and replace the needle in the last 3 or 4 worked loops to maintain consistency and continue working drop stitches for remainder of row (see page 8).

Join with slip stitch as indicated unless otherwise stated.

SPECIAL STITCH

Drop stitch (drop st): Hold knitting needle in non-hook hand close to work with point facing direction of work. Insert hook as indicated, yo, pull lp through, ch 1, extending lp on hook to fit over knitting needle, place lp on needle (see page 4).

JACKET
BACK YOKE & BACK OF SLEEVES

Row 1 (RS): With crochet hook, ch 106 (130), sc in 2nd ch from hook, sc in each rem ch across. *(105 [129] sc)*

Row 2: Holding knitting needle in non-hook hand close to work, ch 1, extending lp to fit over needle, place lp on needle *(first drop st made)*, working in **back lps** *(see Stitch Guide)*, work **drop st** *(see Special Stitch)* in each rem sc across, remove all drop sts. **Do not turn.** *(105 [129] drop sts)*

Row 3: Leaving small length of yarn to match height of drop st (see page 7), insert hook in first drop st, yo, pull lp through, ch 1, sc in same drop st, ch 2, sc through next 3 drop sts at same time, sc in next drop st, sc through next 3 drop sts at same time, *[sc in next drop st, ch 1] 4 times, [sc in next drop st, sc through next 3 drop sts at same time] twice, rep from * across to last drop st, ch 2, sc in last drop st. **Do not turn.**

Row 4: Holding needle in non-hook hand close to work, ch 1, extending lp to fit over needle, place lp on needle, work drop st in each of next 2 chs, working in back lps, work drop st in each sc and ch across to last ch-2 sp, work drop st in each of next 2 chs, work drop st in last sc, remove all drop sts. **Do not turn.** *(105 [129] drop sts)*

Rows 5–16 [5–18]: [Rep rows 3 and 4 alternately] 6 [7] times.

Row 17 [19]: Rep row 3. Fasten off.

FIRST SIDE OF FRONT YOKE & FRONT OF SLEEVE

Row 1: Hold piece with RS facing and foundation ch at top, **join** *(see Pattern Notes)* yarn in first unused lp of foundation ch at left-hand edge *(or at right-hand edge for left-handers)*, holding needle in non-hook hand close to work, ch 1, extending lp to fit over needle, place lp on needle, work drop st in each of next 48 [60] unused lps, work 2 drop sts in each of next 2 lps, remove all drop sts. **Do not turn.** Leave rem lps of foundation ch unworked. *(53 [65] drop sts)*

Row 2: Leaving small length of yarn to match height of drop st, insert hook in first drop st, ch 1, sc in same drop st, ch 2, sc in each of next 3 drop sts, *[sc in next drop st, ch 1] 4 times, [sc in next drop st, sc through next 3 drop sts at same time] twice, rep from * to last drop st, ch 2, sc in last drop st. **Do not turn.**

Row 3: Holding needle in non-hook hand close to work, ch 1, extending lp to fit over needle, place lp on needle, work drop st in each of next 2 chs, working in back lps, work drop st in each sc and ch across to last ch-2 sp, work drop st in each of next 2 chs, work drop st in last sc, remove all drop sts. **Do not turn.** *(57 [69] drop sts)*

Row 4: Leaving small length of yarn to match height of drop st, insert hook in first drop st, ch 1, sc in same drop st, ch 2, sc through next 3 drop sts at same time, sc in next drop st, sc through next 3 drop sts at same time, *[sc in next drop st, ch 1] 4 times, [sc in next drop st, sc through next 3 drop sts at same time] twice, rep from * to last drop st, ch 2, sc in last drop st. **Do not turn.**

Rows 5–24 [5–28]: [Rep rows 3 and 4 alternately] 10 [12] times. At end of last row, fasten off.

2ND SIDE OF FRONT YOKE & FRONT OF SLEEVE

Row 1: With RS facing, sk next 3 unused lps of foundation ch from first side, join yarn in next unused lp, holding needle in non-hook hand close to work, ch 1, extending lp to fit over needle, place lp on needle, work drop st in same st as beg ch-1, work 2 drop sts in next unused lp of ch, *work drop st in each of next 49 [61] unused lps, remove all drop sts. **Do not turn.** *(53 [65] drop sts)*

Row 2: Leaving small length of yarn to match height of drop st, insert hook in first drop st, ch 1, sc in same drop st, ch 2, sc through next 3 drop sts at same time, sc in next drop st, sc through next 3 drop sts at same time, *[sc in next drop st, ch 1] 4 times, [sc in next drop st, sc through next 3 drop sts at same time] twice, rep from * across to last 9 drop sts, [sc in next drop st, ch 1] 4 times, sc in each of next 4 drop sts, ch 2, sc in last drop st. **Do not turn.**

Row 3: Holding needle in non-hook hand close to work, ch 1, extending lp to fit over needle, place lp on needle, work drop st in each of next 2 chs, working in back lps, work drop st in each sc and ch across to last ch-2 sp, work drop st in each of next 2 chs, work drop st in last sc, remove all drop sts. **Do not turn.** *(57 [69] drop sts)*

Row 4: Leaving small length of yarn to match height of drop st, insert hook in first drop st, ch 1, sc in same drop st, ch 2, sc through next 3 drop sts at same time, sc in next drop st, sc through next 3 drop sts at same time, *[sc in next drop st, ch 1] 4 times, [sc in next drop st, sc through next 3 drop sts at same time] twice, rep from * across to last drop st, ch 2, sc in last drop st. **Do not turn.**

Rows 5–24 [5–28]: [Rep rows 3 and 4 alternately] 10 [12] times. At end of last row, fasten off.

BODY JOINING

Row 1: Hold piece with RS facing, join yarn in first sc of last row of first front, ch 1, sc in same sc as beg ch-1, sc in each of next 2 chs, sc in each of next 42 [54] sc, ch 9 (*for underarm*), sk rem sc on front, hold last row of back close to hook, sk first sc, next ch-2 sp and next 9 sc of last row, sc in each of next 81 [105] sc of back, ch 9 (*for underarm*), sk rem sc on back, hold last row of 2nd front close to hook, sk first sc, next ch-2 sp and next 9 sc of last row, sc in each of next 42 [54] sc, sc in each of next 2 chs, sc in last sc. **Do not turn.** (*171 [219] sc, 2 ch-9 sps*)

Row 2: Holding needle in non-hook hand close to work, ch 1, extending lp to fit over needle, place lp on needle, work drop st in each sc and ch across, remove all drop sts. **Do not turn.** (*189 [237] drop sts*)

Row 3: Leaving a small length of yarn to match height of drop st, insert hook in first drop st, ch 1, sc in same drop st, ch 2, sc through next 3 drop sts at same time, sc in next drop st, sc through next 3 drop sts at same time, *[sc in next drop st, ch 1] 4 times, [sc in next drop st, sc through next 3 drop sts at same time] twice, rep from * across to last drop st, ch 2, sc in last drop st. **Do not turn.**

Row 4: Holding needle in non-hook hand close to work, ch 1, extending lp to fit over needle, place lp on needle, work drop st in each of next 2 chs, working in back lps, work drop st in each sc and ch across to last ch-2 sp, work drop st in each of next 2 chs, work drop st in last sc, remove all drop sts. Do not turn. (*189 [237] drop sts*)

Rows 5–20 [5–24]: [Rep rows 3 and 4 alternately] 8 [10] times.

Row 21 [25]: Rep row 3. Fasten off.

EDGING
Row 1: Join yarn in end of last row of Body on one front edge, ch 1, sc in same sp as beg ch-1, sc evenly sp across front edge, back neck edge and next front edge to last row of Body, turn.

Rows 2–5: Ch 1, working in back lps, sc in each sc across, turn. At end of last row, fasten off.

ASSEMBLY
With tapestry needle, sew bottom seam of each Sleeve.

BLOCKING
Immerse project in cool water, squeeze to remove excess water, roll in clean towel to remove as much water as possible, lay flat and shape, stretching out the drop sts to their full height. Allow to dry. ■

Sultana Cap & Scarf

CAP

SKILL LEVEL

INTERMEDIATE

FINISHED SIZE
Adult woman

FINISHED MEASUREMENTS
Circumference: 25 inches above ribbing

Ribbing circumference: 19 inches

Height (including ribbing): 8 inches

MATERIALS

- Plymouth Yarn Baby Alpaca DK light (light worsted) weight baby alpaca yarn (1¾ oz/125 yds/50g per ball): 3 balls #2050 red
- Sizes F/5/3.75mm and H/8/5mm crochet hooks or size needed to obtain gauge
- Size 19 (15mm) desired length knitting needle
- Tapestry needle

GAUGE
With size H hook: 24 sts = 4 inches (blocked); rnds 1–5 = 1½ inches (blocked)

PATTERN NOTES
Project is worked in rounds from bottom of crown to top. Ribbing is worked after crown is completed.

Drop stitches are created left-to-right for right-handers or right-to-left for left-handers.

As the needle becomes full of loops, gently remove the loops and replace the needle in the last 3 or 4 worked loops to maintain consistency and continue working drop stitches for remainder of round (see page 8).

Join with slip stitch as indicated unless otherwise stated.

SPECIAL STITCHES
Drop stitch (drop st): Hold knitting needle in non-hook hand close to work with point facing direction of work. Insert hook as indicated, yo, pull lp through, ch 1, extending lp on hook to fit over needle, place lp on needle (see page 4).

Cross-stitch (cross-st): Sk next 3 drop sts, holding them in front of work, sc in each of next 3 drop sts, sc in each of 3 sk drop sts (see page 8).

Front post half double crochet (fphdc): Yo, insert hook from front to back to front around post of indicated st, yo, draw through st, yo, draw through all 3 lps on hook.

Back post half double crochet (bphdc): Yo, insert hook from back to front to back around post of indicated st, yo, draw through st, yo, draw through all 3 lps on hook.

CAP
CROWN
Rnd 1: With larger crochet hook, ch 151, being careful not to twist ch, **join** (see Pattern Notes) in first ch to form a large ring, ch 1, sc in each ch around, join in first sc. (151 sc)

Rnd 2: Holding knitting needle in non-hook hand close to work, ch 1, extending lp to fit over needle, place lp on needle (first drop st made), working in **back lps** (see Stitch Guide), work **drop st** (see Special Stitches) in each rem sc, remove all drop sts. (151 drop sts)

Rnd 3: Leaving small length of yarn to match height of drop st (see page 7), insert hook in first drop st, yo, pull lp through, ch 1, sc in same drop st, work **cross-st** *(see Special Stitches)* 25 times, join in first sc. *(25 cross-sts, 151 sc)*

Rnds 4 & 5: Rep rnds 2 and 3.

Rnd 6: Rep rnd 2.

Rnd 7: Leaving small length of yarn to match height of drop st, insert hook in first drop st, yo, pull lp through, ch 1, sc in same drop st, *sk next 3 drop sts, holding them in front of work, sc through next 2 drop sts at same time, sc in next drop st, sc in each of 3 sk drop sts, rep from * 24 times, join in first sc. **Do not turn.** *(126 sc)*

Rnd 8: Rep rnd 2.

Rnd 9: Leaving small length of yarn to match height of drop st, insert hook in first drop st, yo, pull lp through, ch 1, sc in same drop st, *sk next 3 drop sts, holding them in front of work, sc in each of next 2 drop sts, sc through first 2 sk drop sts at same time, sc in

3rd sk drop st, rep from * 24 times, join in first sc. **Do not turn.** *(101 sc)*

Rnd 10: Rep rnd 2.

Rnd 11: Leaving small length of yarn to match height of drop st, insert hook in first drop st, yo, pull lp through, ch 1, sc in same drop st, *sk next 2 drop sts, holding them in front of work, sc through next 2 drop sts at same time, sc in each of 2 sk drop sts, rep from * 24 times, join in first sc. **Do not turn.** *(76 sc)*

Rnd 12: Rep rnd 2.

Rnd 13: Leaving small length of yarn to match height of drop st, insert hook in first drop st, yo, pull lp through, ch 1, sc in same drop st, *sk next 2 drop sts, holding them in front of work, sc in next drop st, sc through 2 sk drop sts at same time, rep from * 24 times, join in first sc. **Do not turn.** *(51 sc)*

Rnd 14: Ch 1, sk first sc, [**sc dec** *(see Stitch Guide)* in next 2 sc, sc in each of next 8 sc] 5 times, join in first sc. *(45 sc)*

Rnd 15: Ch 1, sc dec in first 2 sc, sc in each of next 7 sc, [sc dec in next 2 sc, sc in each of next 7 sc] 4 times, join in first sc. *(40 sc)*

Rnd 16: Ch 1, sc dec in first 2 sc, sc in each of next 6 sc, [sc dec in next 2 sc, sc in each of next 6 sc] 4 times, join in first sc. *(35 sc)*

Rnd 17: Ch 1, sc dec in first 2 sc, sc in each of next 5 sc, [sc dec in next 2 sc, sc in each of next 5 sc] 4 times, join in first sc. *(30 sc)*

Rnd 18: Ch 1, sc dec in first 2 sc, sc in each of next 4 sc, [sc dec in next 2 sc, sc in each of next 4 sc] 4 times, join in first sc. *(25 sc)*

Rnd 19: Ch 1, sc dec in first 2 sc, sc in each of next 3 sc, [sc dec in next 2 sc, sc in each of next 3 sc] 4 times, join in first sc. *(20 sc)*

Rnd 20: Ch 1, sc dec in first 2 sc, sc in each of next 2 sc, [sc dec in next 2 sc, sc in each of next 2 sc] 4 times, join in first sc. *(15 sc)*

Rnd 21: Ch 1, sc dec in first 2 sc, sc in next sc, [sc dec in next 2 sc, sc in next sc] 4 times, join in first sc. *(10 sc)*

Rnd 22: Ch 1, sc dec in first 2 sc, [sc dec in next 2 sc] 4 times, join in first sc. Leaving 7-inch tail, fasten off. *(5 sc)*

ASSEMBLY
With tapestry needle, weave tail through tops of each of 5 sc, gather to close opening and secure.

RIBBING
Rnd 1: Hold piece with foundation ch at top, with smaller crochet hook, join yarn in any unused lp on opposite side of foundation ch, ch 1, work 98 hdc evenly sp around, join in first hdc. *(98 hdc)*

Rnd 2: Ch 1, **fphdc** *(see Special Stitches)* around same st as joining, **bphdc** *(see Special Stitches)* around next st, *fphdc around next st, bphdc around next st, rep from * around, join in first fphdc.

Rnds 3–5: Rep rnd 2. At end of last rnd, fasten off.

BLOCKING
Immerse project in cool water, squeeze to remove excess water, roll in clean towel to remove as much water as possible, lay flat and shape, stretching out the drop sts to their full height. Allow to dry.

SCARF

SKILL LEVEL
■■□□
EASY

FINISHED MEASUREMENTS
6½ x 60 inches

MATERIALS
- Plymouth Yarn Baby Alpaca DK light (light worsted) weight baby alpaca yarn (1¾ oz/125 yds/50g per ball): 3 balls #2050 red
- Size H/8/5mm crochet hook or size needed to obtain gauge
- Size 19 (15mm) desired length knitting needle
- Tapestry needle

GAUGE
5 sc = 1 inch (blocked); 4 cross-sts = 4 inches (blocked); rows 1–3 = 1½ inches (blocked)

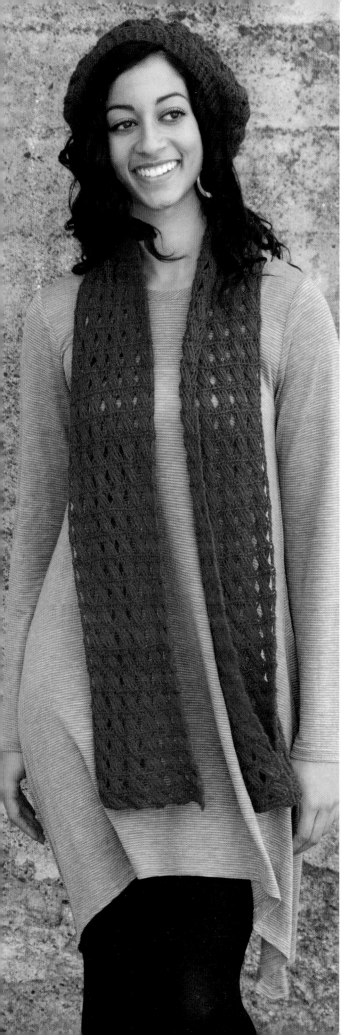

PATTERN NOTES

Drop stitches are created left-to-right for right-handers or right-to-left for left-handers.

Weave in ends as work progresses.

SPECIAL STITCHES

Drop stitch (drop st): Hold knitting needle in non-hook hand close to work with point facing direction of work. Insert hook in indicated st, yo, pull lp through, ch 1, extending lp on hook to fit over knitting needle, place lp on needle (see page 4).

Cross-stitch (cross-st): Sk next 3 drop sts, holding them in front of work, sc in each of next 3 drop sts, sc in each of 3 sk drop sts (see page 8).

SCARF

Row 1: With crochet hook, ch 39, sc in 2nd ch from hook, sc in each rem ch across. **Do not turn.** (38 sc)

Row 2: Holding needle in non-hook hand close to work, ch 1, extending lp to fit over needle, place lp on needle (first drop st made), working in **back lps** (see Stitch Guide), work **drop st** (see Special Stitches) in each rem sc across, remove all drop sts, **do not turn.** (38 drop sts)

Row 3: Leaving small length of yarn to match height of drop st (see page 7), insert hook in first drop st, yo, pull lp through, ch 1, sc in same drop st, [**cross-st** (see Special Stitches)] 6 times, sc in last drop st. **Do not turn.** (6 cross-sts)

Rows 4–117: [Rep rows 2 and 3 consecutively] 57 times. At end of last row, fasten off.

BLOCKING

Immerse project in cool water, squeeze to remove excess water, roll in clean towel to remove as much water as possible, lay flat and shape, stretching out the drop sts to their full height. Allow to dry. ■

Lynden *Scarf*

SKILL LEVEL

■■□□
EASY

FINISHED MEASUREMENTS
8 x 50 inches

MATERIALS
- Universal Yarn Renew Wool light (light worsted) weight wool yarn (3½ oz/270 yds/100g per skein): 1 skein #102 husk
- Size I/9/5.5mm crochet hook or size needed to obtain gauge
- Size 19 (15mm) desired length knitting needle
- Tapestry needle

GAUGE
12 sc = 4 inches (blocked); rows 1–5 = 1½ inches (blocked)

PATTERN NOTES
Scarf is worked lengthwise.

If you would prefer to learn the technique with a fewer number of stitches, use this pattern and work the scarf widthwise rather than lengthwise with a foundation chain of about 28 to begin. Continue in stitch pattern for the desired length.

Drop stitches are created left-to-right for right-handers or right-to-left for left-handers.

As the knitting needle becomes full of loops, gently remove the loops and replace the needle in the last 3 or 4 worked loops to maintain consistency and continue working drop stitches for remainder of row (see page 8).

SPECIAL STITCH
Drop stitch (drop st): Hold knitting needle in non-hook hand close to work with point facing direction of work. Insert hook in indicated st, yo, pull lp through, ch 1, extending lp on hook to fit over knitting needle, place lp on needle (see page 4).

SCARF
Row 1: With crochet hook, ch 151, sc in 2nd ch from hook, sc in each rem ch across, turn. *(150 sc)*

Row 2: Ch 1, sc in each st across, turn.

Row 3: Ch 1, sc in each sc across. **Do not turn.**

Row 4: Holding knitting needle in non-hook hand close to work, ch 1, extend lp on hook to fit over needle and place on needle *(first drop st made)*, work **drop st** *(see Special Stitch)* in each rem sc across, remove all drop sts from needle. **Do not turn.** *(150 drop sts)*

Row 5: Leaving small length of yarn to match height of drop st (see page 7), insert hook in first drop st, yo, pull lp through, ch 1, sc in same drop st, sc in each rem drop st across, turn. *(150 sc)*

Rows 6–9: Rep rows 2–5.

Rows 10–21: [Rep rows 6–9 consecutively] 3 times.

Rows 22 & 23: Rep row 2.

Rnd 24: Ch 1, now working around outer edge, work sc evenly sp around, with 3 sc at each corner, join with sl st in first sc. Fasten off.

BLOCKING
Immerse project in cool water, squeeze to remove excess water, roll in clean towel to remove as much water as possible, lie flat and shape, stretching out the drop sts to their full height. Allow to dry. ■

Madeira *Wrap*

SKILL LEVEL

■■■□

INTERMEDIATE

FINISHED MEASUREMENTS

17 inches x 56 inches at widest points

MATERIALS

- Classic Elite Yarns Magnolia light (light worsted) weight merino wool/ silk yarn (1¾ oz/120 yds/50g per ball): 3 balls #5456 plum
- Size J/10/6mm crochet hook or size needed to obtain gauge
- Size 19 (15mm) desired length knitting needle
- Tapestry needle

GAUGE

In pattern: 13 sts = 4 inches (blocked); rows 1–5 = 2 inches (blocked)

PATTERN NOTES

Drop stitches are created left-to-right for right-handers or right-to-left for left-handers.

As the knitting needle becomes full of loops, gently remove the loops and replace the needle in the last 3 or 4 worked loops to maintain consistency and continue working drop stitches across remainder of row (see page 8).

Join with slip stitch as indicated unless otherwise stated.

SPECIAL STITCH

Drop stitch (drop st): Hold knitting needle in non-hook hand close to work with point facing direction of work. Insert hook as indicated, yo, pull lp through, ch 1, extending lp on hook to fit over knitting needle, place lp on needle (see page 4).

WRAP

CENTER

Row 1: Beg at top edge with crochet hook, ch 186, sc in 2nd ch from hook, sc in each rem ch across. **Do not turn.** *(185 sc)*

Row 2: Holding knitting needle in non-hook hand close to work, ch 1, extending lp to fit over needle, place lp on needle *(first drop st made)*, work **drop st** *(see Special Stitch)* in each rem sc across, remove all drop sts. **Do not turn.** *(185 drop sts)*

Row 3: Leaving small length of yarn to match height of drop st (see page 7), insert hook through next 5 drop sts , yo, pull lp through all 5 drop sts, ch 1, sc through same 5 drop sts at same time, [sc in each of next 5 drop sts, ch 2, sc through next 5 drop sts at same time, ch 2] 17 times, sc in each of next 5 drop sts, sc through next 5 drop sts at same time. **Do not turn.** *(177 sts)*

Row 4: Rep row 2. *(177 drop sts)*

Row 5: Leaving small length of yarn to match height of drop st, insert hook through next 6 drop sts, yo, pull lp through 6 drop sts, ch 1, sc through same 6 drop sts at same time, [sc in each of next 5 drop sts, ch 2, sc through next 5 drop sts at same time, ch 2] across to last 11 drop sts, sc in each of next 5 drop sts, sc through next 6 drop sts at same time. **Do not turn.** *(167 sts)*

Rows 6–35: [Rep rows 4 and 5 alternately] 15 times. *(17 sts at end of last row)*

Row 36: Rep row 4. *(17 drop sts)*

Row 37: Leaving small length of yarn to match height of drop st, insert hook though next 6 drop sts, yo, pull lp through same 6 drop sts, ch 1, sc through same 6 drop sts at same time, sc in each of next 5 drop sts, ch 2, sc through next 6 drop sts at same time. **Do not turn.** *(7 sc)*

Row 38: Rep row 4. *(7 drop sts)*

Row 39: Leaving small length of yarn to match height of drop st, insert hook through next 7 drop sts, yo, pull through same 7 drop sts, ch 1, sc through same 7 drop sts at same time. Fasten off.

TRIM
Note: Trim is worked on 2 side edges only.

Row 1 (RS): Hold Center with top edge to right, with crochet hook, **join** *(see Pattern Notes)* yarn in end of row 1 in right-hand corner *(or left-hand corner for left-handers)* of Center,

*ch 8, sc in 4th ch from hook *(ch-3 sp made)*, hdc in next ch, dc in next ch, tr in next ch, **dtr** *(see Stitch Guide)* in last ch, sl st in end of next row, rep from * to tip, working across next side, **ch 8, sc in 4th ch from hook *(ch-3 sp made)*, hdc in next ch, dc in next ch, tr in next ch, dtr in last ch, sl st in end of next row, rep from ** across to row 1 of Center. Fasten off.

Row 2: Hold piece with WS facing, join yarn in first ch-3 sp, ch 1, sc in same sp, [ch 9, sc in next ch-3 sp] across, turn.

Row 3: Ch 1, sc in first sc, [3 sc, ch 6, sl st in 3rd ch from hook, ch 3, 3 sc] in each ch-9 sp across, sc in last sc. Fasten off.

BLOCKING
Immerse project in cool water, squeeze to remove excess water, roll in clean towel to remove as much water as possible, lay flat and shape, stretching out the drop sts to their full height. Allow to dry. ∎

Einset Tank Top

SKILL LEVEL

■□□□
EXPERIENCED

FINISHED SIZES

Instructions given fit 32–34-inch bust (*small*); changes for 36–38-inch bust (*medium*), 40–42-inch bust (*large*), 44–46-inch bust (*X-large*), 48–50-inch bust (*2X-large*) and 52–54-inch bust (*3X-large*) are in [ ].

MATERIALS

- Plymouth Yarn Cleo light (light worsted) weight mercerized cotton yarn (1¾ oz/125 yds/50g per skein): 5 (6, 6, 7, 8, 9) skeins #110 solar
- Sizes F/5/3.75mm and H/8/5mm crochet hooks or size needed to obtain gauge
- Size 17 (12.75mm) desired length knitting needle
- Tapestry needle

GAUGE

With size H: 14 sc = 4 inches (blocked); 14 rows = 4 inches (blocked)

PATTERN NOTES

Bodice is made, bottom up, in two pieces and then seamed at shoulders and sides. Stitches are picked up along the lower edge and worked from top down in rounds.

Cotton yarn can get heavy. Expect two or more inches of growth in the bodice alone. There will also be growth in the skirting. When blocking the bodice, smooth it from top to bottom vertically while wet, even shaking it down while wet, in order to mimic the effects of gravity.

Drop stitches are created left-to-right for right-handers or right-to-left for left-handers.

As the knitting needle becomes full of loops, gently remove the loops and replace the needle in the last 3 or 4 worked loops to maintain consistency and continue working drop stitches for remainder of row (see page 8).

Join with slip stitch as indicated unless otherwise stated.

SPECIAL STITCH

Drop stitch (drop st): Hold knitting needle in non-hook hand close to work with point facing direction of work. Insert hook as indicated, yo, pull lp through, ch 1, extending lp on hook to fit over knitting needle, place lp on needle (see page 4).

TANK TOP
BACK BODICE

Row 1: With larger crochet hook, ch 60 [68, 74, 82, 88, 96]), sc in 2nd ch from hook and in each rem ch across, turn. (*59 [67, 73, 81, 87, 95] sc*)

Rows 2–8: Ch 1, sc in each sc across, turn.

Row 9: Sl st in each of first 4 [5, 6, 7, 8, 9] sc, ch 1, sc in each of next 51 [57, 61, 67, 71, 77] sc, turn, leaving rem 4 [5, 6, 7, 8, 9] sc unworked. (*51 [57, 61, 67, 71, 77] sc*)

Row 10: Ch 1, sk first sc, sc in each sc across to last 2 sc, sk next sc, sc in last sc, turn. (*49 [55, 59, 65, 69, 75] sc*)

Rows 11–13 [11–13, 11–13, 11–15, 11–16, 11–19]: Rep row 10. (*43 [49, 53, 55, 57, 57] sc at end of last row*)

Rows 14–33 [14–35, 14–35, 16–37, 17–37, 20–39]: Ch 1, sc in each sc across, turn.

FIRST SHOULDER

Row 1: Ch 1, sc in each of first 6 [8, 9, 9, 9, 9] sc, turn, leaving rem 37 [41, 44, 46, 48, 48] sc unworked. (6 [8, 9, 9, 9, 9] sc)

Rows 2–4: Ch 1, sc in each sc across, turn. At end of last row, fasten off.

2ND SHOULDER

Row 1: Sk next 31 [33, 35, 37, 39, 39] unworked sc from First Shoulder, **join** (see Pattern Notes) yarn in next sc, ch 1, sc in same sc as beg ch-1, sc in each rem sc across, turn. (6 [8, 9, 9, 9, 9] sc)

Rows 2–4: Ch 1, sc in each sc across, turn. At end of last row, fasten off.

FRONT BODICE

Row 1: With larger crochet hook, ch 60 [68, 74, 82, 88, 96], sc in 2nd ch from hook, sc in each rem ch across, turn. (59 [67, 73, 81, 87, 95] sc)

Rows 2–8: Ch 1, sc in each sc across, turn.

Row 9: Sl st in each of first 4 [5, 6, 7, 8, 9] sc, ch 1, sc in each of next 51 [57, 61, 67, 71, 77] sc, turn, leaving rem 4 [5, 6, 7, 8, 9] sc unworked. (51 [57, 61, 67, 71, 77] sc)

Row 10: Ch 1, sk first sc, sc in each sc across to last 2 sc, sk next sc, sc in last sc, turn. (49 [55, 59, 65, 69, 75] sc)

Rows 11–14 [11–14, 11–14, 11–16, 11–17, 11–20]: Rep row 10. (41 [47, 51, 53, 55, 55] sc at end of last row)

Rows 15–24 [15–24, 15–24, 17–26, 18–24, 21–26]: Ch 1, sc in each sc across, turn.

FIRST SHOULDER

Row 1: Ch 1, sc in each of first 16 [18, 19, 19, 19, 19] sc, turn, leaving rem 25 [29, 32, 34, 36, 36] sc unworked. (16 [18, 19, 19, 19, 19] sc)

Row 2: Sl st in each of first 4 sc, ch 1, sc in each rem sc across, turn. (12 [14, 15, 15, 15, 15] sc)

Row 3: Ch 1, sc in each of first 8 [10, 11, 11, 11, 11] sc, turn, leaving rem 4 sc unworked. (8 [10, 11, 11, 11, 11] sc)

Row 4: Ch 1, sk first sc, sc in each rem sc across, turn. (7 [9, 10, 10, 10, 10] sc)

Row 5: Ch 1, sc in each sc across to last 2 sc, sk next sc, sc in last sc, turn. (6 [8, 9, 9, 9, 9] sc)

Rows 6–14 [6–16, 6–16, 6–16, 6–18, 6–18]: Ch 1, sc in each sc across, turn. At end of last row, fasten off.

2ND SHOULDER

Row 1: Sk next 9 [11, 13, 15, 17, 17] sc from First Shoulder, join yarn in next sc, ch 1, sc in same sc as beg ch-1, sc in each rem sc across, turn. (16 [18, 19, 19, 19, 19] sc)

Row 2: Ch 1, sc in each of first 12 [14, 15, 15, 15, 15] sc, turn, leaving rem 4 sc unworked. (12 [14, 15, 15, 15, 15] sc)

Row 3: Sl st in each of first 4 sc, ch 1, sc in same sc as beg ch-1, sc in each rem sc across, turn. (8 [10, 11, 11, 11, 11] sc)

Row 4: Ch 1, sc in each sc across to last 2 sc, sk next sc, sc in last sc, turn. (7 [9, 10, 10, 10, 10] sc)

Row 5: Ch 1, sk first sc, sc in each rem sc across, turn. (6 [8, 9, 9, 9, 9] sc)

Rows 6–14 [6–16, 6–16, 6–16, 6–18, 6–18]: Ch 1, sc in each sc across, turn. At end of last row, fasten off.

ASSEMBLY

With tapestry needle, sew shoulder seams and side seams.

SKIRTING

Rnd 1: Hold piece with Back Bodice facing and foundation ch at top, working in unused lps on opposite side of foundation ch with larger hook, join yarn in ch at center back, ch 1, sc in same ch as beg ch-1, [ch 3, sk next 2 chs, sc, ch 4, sk next 2 chs, sc in next ch] 19 [22, 24, 26, 28, 31] times, ch 3, sk next 3 [1, 1, 5, 5, 3] ch(s), join in first sc. (39 [45, 49, 53, 57, 63] ch sps)

Rnd 2: Holding knitting needle in non-hook hand close to work, ch 1, extending lp to fit over needle, place lp on needle (*first drop st made*), sl st in same sc, *ch 7, sk ch-3 sp, (sl st, 10 **drop sts**—*see Special Stitch*, sl st) in next ch-4 sp, rep from * to last ch-3 sp, ch 7, sk ch-3 sp, (sl st, drop st) in same sc as beg ch-1 (*there will be 2 drop sts in same sc as beg ch-1*), remove all drop sts. **Do not turn.** (*192 [222, 242, 262, 282, 312] drop sts*)

Rnd 3: Leaving small length of yarn to match height of drop st (see page 7), remove hook, insert hook in first and last drop sts at same time, yo, pull lp through 2 drop sts, ch 1, sc through same 2 drop sts at same time, *sc in next ch-7 sp, [sc through next 2 drop sts at same time, ch 1] 4 times, sc through next 2 drop sts at same time, rep from * to last ch-7 sp, sc in last ch-7 sp, join in first sc.

Rnd 4: Ch 1, sc in same sc as beg ch-1, ch 4, *sc in next ch-1 sp, ch 4, sk next 2 ch-1 sps, sc in next ch-1 sp, ch 4, rep from * around, join in first sc.

Rnds 5–22 [5–25, 5–25, 5–28, 5–28, 5–28]: [Rep rnds 2–4 consecutively] 6 [7, 7, 8, 8, 8] times.

Rnds 23 & 24 [26 & 27, 26 & 27, 29 & 30, 29 & 30, 29 & 30]: Rep rnds 2 and 3. At end of last rnd, fasten off.

NECKLINE EDGING

With smaller hook, join yarn in one shoulder seam, ch 1, sc in same sp as beg ch-1, sc evenly sp around neckline, join in first sc. Fasten off.

ARMHOLE EDGING

With smaller hook, join yarn in side seam on one armhole, ch 1, sc in same sp as beg ch-1, sc evenly sp around armhole, join in first sc. Fasten off.

Rep on 2nd armhole.

BLOCKING

Immerse project in cool water, squeeze to remove excess water, roll in clean towel to remove as much water as possible, lay flat and shape, stretching out the drop sts to their full height. Allow to dry. ■

Perlette
Cowl

SKILL LEVEL

EASY

FINISHED MEASUREMENTS

10 inches wide x 40 inches in circumference at top, 50 inches in circumference at bottom

MATERIALS

- Universal Yarn Rozetti Polaris light (light worsted) weight acrylic/wool/payette yarn (1¾ oz/192 yds/50g per ball):
    1 ball #61003 cloud dancer
- Size J/10/6mm crochet hook or size needed to obtain gauge
- Size 19 (15mm) desired length knitting needle
- Tapestry needle

GAUGE

12 sc = 4 inches (blocked); rnds 1–3 = 1½ inches (blocked)

PATTERN NOTES

Project is worked in rounds.

Drop stitches are created left-to-right for right-handers or right-to-left for left-handers.

As the knitting needle becomes full of loops, gently remove the loops and replace the needle in the last 3 or 4 worked loops to maintain consistency and continue working drop stitches for remainder of round (see page 8).

The yarn includes sequins worked directly into the yarn strands. When you encounter a sequin, you may need to work a little more loosely in order to pull the loops through the stitches.

Join with slip stitch as indicated unless otherwise stated.

SPECIAL STITCH

Drop stitch (drop st): Hold knitting needle in non-hook hand close to work with point facing direction of work. Insert hook in indicated st,

yo, pull lp through, ch 1, extending lp on hook to fit over knitting needle, place lp on needle (see page 4).

COWL

Rnd 1: With crochet hook, ch 150, being careful not to twist ch, **join** (see Pattern Notes) in first ch to form a large ring, ch 1, sc in each ch around, join in first sc.

Rnd 2: Holding knitting needle in non-hook hand close to work, ch 1, extending lp on hook to fit over needle, place lp on needle (first drop st made), work **drop st** (see Special Stitch) in each rem sc, remove all drop sts, **do not turn**. (150 drop sts)

Rnd 3: Insert crochet hook in first drop st, turn 360 degrees (see page 9), leaving small length of yarn to match height of drop st (see page 7), yo, pull lp through, ch 1, sc in same drop st, *insert hook in next drop st, twist 360 degrees, sc in same drop st, rep from * around, join in first sc.

Rnds 4 & 5: Rep rnds 2 and 3.

Rnd 6: Ch 1, sk first sc, sc in each of next 9 sc, [sk next sc, sc in each of next 9 sc] 14 times, join in first sc. (135 sc)

Rnd 7: Ch 1, sc in each sc around, join in first sc.

Rnds 8–11: Rep rnds 2–5.

Rnd 12: Ch 1, sk first sc, sc in each of next 8 sc, [sk next sc, sc in each of next 8 sc] 14 times, join in first sc. (120 sc)

Rnd 13: Ch 1, sc in each sc around, join in first sc.

Rnds 14–17: Rep rnds 2–5.

Rnd 18: Ch 1, sc in each sc around, join in first sc. Fasten off.

BLOCKING

Immerse project in cool water, squeeze to remove excess water, roll in clean towel to remove as much water as possible, lay flat and shape, stretching out the drop sts to their full height. Allow to dry. ■

Annie's® *Learn Drop Stitch Crochet* is published by Annie's, 306 East Parr Road, Berne, IN 46711. Printed in USA. Copyright © 2013 Annie's. All rights reserved. This publication may not be reproduced in part or in whole without written permission from the publisher.

RETAIL STORES: If you would like to carry this pattern book or any other Annie's publication, visit AnniesWSL.com

Every effort has been made to ensure that the instructions in this pattern book are complete and accurate. We cannot, however, take responsibility for human error, typographical mistakes or variations in individual work. Please visit AnniesCustomerCare.com to check for pattern updates.

ISBN: 978-1-59635-855-3

1 2 3 4 5 6 7 8 9

STITCH GUIDE

FOR MORE COMPLETE INFORMATION, VISIT **ANNIESCATALOG.COM/STITCHGUIDE**

STITCH ABBREVIATIONS

beg	begin/begins/beginning
bpdc	back post double crochet
bpsc	back post single crochet
bptr	back post treble crochet
CC	contrasting color
ch(s)	chain(s)
ch-	refers to chain or space previously made (i.e., ch-1 space)
ch sp(s)	chain space(s)
cl(s)	cluster(s)
cm	centimeter(s)
dc	double crochet (singular/plural)
dc dec	double crochet 2 or more stitches together, as indicated
dec	decrease/decreases/decreasing
dtr	double treble crochet
ext	extended
fpdc	front post double crochet
fpsc	front post single crochet
fptr	front post treble crochet
g	gram(s)
hdc	half double crochet
hdc dec	half double crochet 2 or more stitches together, as indicated
inc	increase/increases/increasing
lp(s)	loop(s)
MC	main color
mm	millimeter(s)
oz	ounce(s)
pc	popcorn(s)
rem	remain/remains/remaining
rep(s)	repeat(s)
rnd(s)	round(s)
RS	right side
sc	single crochet (singular/plural)
sc dec	single crochet 2 or more stitches together, as indicated
sk	skip/skipped/skipping
sl st(s)	slip stitch(es)
sp(s)	space(s)/spaced
st(s)	stitch(es)
tog	together
tr	treble crochet
trtr	triple treble
WS	wrong side
yd(s)	yard(s)
yo	yarn over

YARN CONVERSION

OUNCES TO GRAMS		GRAMS TO OUNCES	
1	28.4	25	7/8
2	56.7	40	1 2/3
3	85.0	50	1 3/4
4	113.4	100	3 1/2

UNITED STATES		UNITED KINGDOM
sl st (slip stitch)	=	sc (single crochet)
sc (single crochet)	=	dc (double crochet)
hdc (half double crochet)	=	htr (half treble crochet)
dc (double crochet)	=	tr (treble crochet)
tr (treble crochet)	=	dtr (double treble crochet)
dtr (double treble crochet)	=	ttr (triple treble crochet)
skip	=	miss

Single crochet decrease (sc dec):
(Insert hook, yo, draw lp through) in each of the sts indicated, yo, draw through all lps on hook.

Example of 2-sc dec

Half double crochet decrease (hdc dec):
(Yo, insert hook, yo, draw lp through) in each of the sts indicated, yo, draw through all lps on hook.

Example of 2-hdc dec

Reverse single crochet (reverse sc):
Ch 1, sk first st, working from left to right, insert hook in next st from front to back, draw up lp on hook, yo and draw through both lps on hook.

Chain (ch):
Yo, pull through lp on hook.

Single crochet (sc):
Insert hook in st, yo, pull through st, yo, pull through both lps on hook.

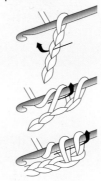

Double crochet (dc):
Yo, insert hook in st, yo, pull through st, [yo, pull through 2 lps] twice.

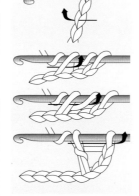

Double crochet decrease (dc dec):
(Yo, insert hook, yo, draw lp through, yo, draw through 2 lps on hook) in each of the sts indicated, yo, draw through all lps on hook.

Example of 2-dc dec

Front loop (front lp) Back loop (back lp)

Front Loop   Back Loop

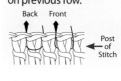

Front post stitch (fp): Back post stitch (bp):
When working post st, insert hook from right to left around post of st on previous row.

Back   Front

Post of Stitch

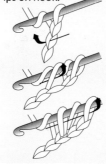

Half double crochet (hdc):
Yo, insert hook in st, yo, pull through st, yo, pull through all 3 lps on hook.

Double treble crochet (dtr):
Yo 3 times, insert hook in st, yo, pull through st, [yo, pull through 2 lps] 4 times.

Treble crochet decrease (tr dec):
Holding back last lp of each st, tr in each of the sts indicated, yo, pull through all lps on hook.

Example of 2-tr dec

Slip stitch (sl st):
Insert hook in st, pull through both lps on hook.

Chain color change (ch color change)
Yo with new color, draw through last lp on hook.

Double crochet color change (dc color change)
Drop first color, yo with new color, draw through last 2 lps of st.

Treble crochet (tr):
Yo twice, insert hook in st, yo, pull through st, [yo, pull through 2 lps] 3 times.

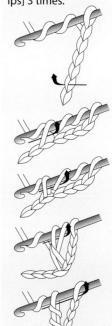